MW01277888

Progress not Perfection

A Millennial's Story

Guided Journal

Personal Development.

Goal Setting.

Achieving Success.

Dr. Lisa Wisniewski

Printed by Kindle Direct Publishing
in the United States of America.

Second printing, 2019.

Amazon
Kindle Direct Publishing

www.bellesnotebook.com

Edited by Dr. John Kania
Designed by Yelena Zinchenko

This book is dedicated to my husband Peter.

*Baby, thank you for your unwavering support -
without you this book would not have been possible.*

*Thank you for understanding my dreams
and for standing by my side as I achieve them.*

CONTENTS

Introduction

Thank you for your purchase of *Progress Not Perfection: A Millennial's Story!* My hope is the book inspires you, helps you set goals, and leads you to live your best life. Before you jump into the pages ahead of you, I wanted to give you some of the background story of this guided journal.

The idea for *Progress not Perfection: A Millennial's Story* came to me in 2015. I wanted to write a book, based on lived experience, that was also interactive for the reader and where they can work on their own goals. I started outlines, writing to publishers, and the first draft. Then the realities of graduate school (I was a student in a doctorate of educational leadership program at the time) sunk in and my focus went towards finishing my degree. Right after graduation I started planning my wedding. All of my fancy outlines, drafts, and letters to publishers remained files on my computer for a few years.

After the wedding, the desire to finish this book started to pop up. I could no longer ignore it and my husband encouraged me to finish it. I looked at the files again and thought I could pick up where I left off. I was wrong. I was a different person. So much of my life had changed. I was also the person that everyone seeks advice from. I started to listen to common themes and realized where the needs are.

The editing began. The idea was the same but the direction was going to be a bit different. The chapters became a shorter, there were more journal prompts, and the topics of the chapters changed. It began to feel like a resource that people can use and needed.

Here we are, 3 years and several life changes later. This is the product of 12 years of graduate school and countless life experiences (personal and professional). This guided journal is part my journey and part your journey. Each chapter is focused on a different part of everyday life. The goal is to think about each part and develop goals for your future.

The stories that I included from my life are meant to be relatable and to inspire thinking about your own story. In the pages ahead, please feel free to interact with them as you wish such as drawing, writing, or highlighting. It is your book, get the most out of it.

Happy reading and journaling!

Please feel free to share your
Progress not Perfection story with me!

I want to hear from you!

Email: drbellesnotebook@gmail.com

Connect & Share your photos with me
Instagram, Facebook, Twitter:
@BellesNotebook

Relationship with Self

The next chapters focus on
your relationship with yourself.

CHAPTER ONE

Balance

I wish I could tell you that I live a life with perfect balance. I wish I could tell you that all my time management and organizational skills lead me to creating the life I want to have daily. I wish I could tell you that as a couple without children, our weeknights and weekends are filled with fun activities of our choosing. If I told you that, I would be lying.

The reason I would be lying to you is because life happens. As much as I can plan my day there are so many unexpected things that can happen. I have had family members that have suddenly gotten sick, new projects that have a faster deadline, and nephew's soccer games that we find out about at the last minute. That is all part of living and adult life.

My point here is not that I do not have total control over my life. I can choose what events I pay attention to and which ones I say no to. I say this to take the pressure off of finding a perfectly balanced life. I found that striving for perfect balance was like running a race with no finish line. It is simply because we cannot plan every detail of our lives. The key part is finding a good middle ground.

I have to say I learned this through extremes. I have a habit of taking on too many things (projects, tasks). I always get things accomplished, but I also get overwhelmed in the process. The following is my journey in finding balance.

As a graduate student, I learned and loved the art of time management. Full disclosure, planners have been my thing since middle school. I did not need much convincing to use one throughout college and graduate school. I did refine my time management skills in graduate school because I was working, going to school, and planning a major conference (in the beginning of my journey). I quickly adapted time blocking of my schedule. It worked for me, and I was able to accomplish all of my school tasks. My only problem here was, I was not adding self-care time into my time blocking. It was all work. During this stage of my life, I was significantly out of balance.

I realized this in late, 2013. That was the year that I finished my master's program, began my doctoral program, and ran an international conference. All of those things happened by August. I was on the go all the time. I had poor sleeping and eating habits. On the last day of the conference, when all was completed, I nearly fainted. Someone caught me and I came too before I collapsed. In the following weeks, I felt simply exhausted, like I could not get enough sleep. I went to the doctor. His advice was simply to rest. I was too exhausted for anything else and my body needed to rest first before I did. I rested for three weeks. I did not know what to do with myself.

After my restful period, the new semester began. I was a full-time student and three weeks later, I left for Poland for a cultural exchange. To be honest, my body was probably not ready for the trip, but I went. I do not regret the decision, but I probably should have listened to my body a bit more.

Throughout the rest of my doctoral program, I continued to have little balance in my life. I was always working on homework assignments, research projects, or going to work. I had some time with friends but by then, everyone had moved in a different direction. My friends were buying homes and having children. I was a full-time student. We had less and less to talk about.

Towards the end of my graduate school journey, I met Peter. Initially, he got my attention by reminding me to celebrate things. This was after a conversation where I told him I did not celebrate anything (including my birthday) and he was appalled by that notion. He did not understand why I would not celebrate the big and small wins of life. I began to listen to him.

I have to say, in the beginning of our relationship, I really wanted to create balance to spend time with him, but I had no idea how to achieve it. Peter was very helpful in this process especially through his constant reminders that I slow down. After six years of going at a fast speed, I could not comprehend let along act in a way that slowed me down.

This was also during the time I was writing my dissertation. A dissertation is a lot of work and typically takes years to complete. I was ready to complete it, and I was really passionate about my research topic. I worked many years to get to this point in my educational career. I was ready, but I had to learn how to balance a major project, work full time, and be in a new relationship.

I believe that Peter, as a supportive partner, was a key to all of this. He was understanding and took on a lot of the tasks like housework or cooking. This is where I learned that a part of balance is acknowledging and asking for help. Before this point, I thought I had to do everything. I put a lot of pressure on myself. Now, I had a partner who was willing to split the work. While I was thrilled, there were plenty of behavioral adjustments to be made on my part. It honestly took me about a year to get used to the fact that he was here, he was not going to leave, and he was sincere about helping.

I will say that my adjustment to not doing it all is a continual work in progress. As the oldest child who was always expected to accomplish tasks, this is undoing thirty plus years of behavior. I am thrilled at my progress yet mature enough to know I will still make mistakes. This is also an ongoing conversation in our relationship.

Since that time, we have been actively working towards and seeking balance. As a couple, we have become very intentional with how we spend our time. There are certain days of the week that we keep for ourselves. We try to keep weekends open so that we can spend time together. It does not work every weekend because sometimes we have to go to work, have family engagements, and want to spend time with our friends. If this does happen, we look for time during the week to spend some quality time.

I can tell you that some weeks this works well and others I want more time but it is not always possible. With this approach towards balance, it has helped me with taking the pressure off and not always feeling like I am failing by not finding it. I look at balance as an ongoing process that is somewhat subjective. It is subjective to time of year (some times of the year are a bit busier than others), family circumstances, and daily occurrences of life. While I still ultimately have control over my life and my choices, I allow life to unfold as it should.

Balance

TIPS & TRICKS

Ask for help

YOU DO NOT HAVE TO DO IT ALL.

Ask for help and delegate tasks. This will help create more time to do the things that you would like to do. Also, your time is valuable and treat it as such.

Seek Progress not Perfection

BALANCE IS AN ONGOING PROCESS

There will be times where you can achieve this goal and other times where it will not be so easy. Be ok with that process and understand it is a part of life. Do not put pressure on to be in perfect balance all the time.

WORKSHEET

Feel free to answer the questions in a way you feel comfortable (ex. writing, drawing). *Get creative!*

. . . .

Life is like riding a bicycle.
To keep your balance, you must keep moving.
- Albert Einstein

. . . .

How will you achieve balance in your life?
(ex. work less, ask for help, find self-care time)

_____

_____

_____

Why is this important to you?

_____

_____

_____

How close are you to achieving your goals for balance?

_____

_____

_____

NOTEBOOK

Belle's

Lisa Wisniewski

Health, Beauty and Lifestyle
Blog

www.bellesnotebook.com
drbellesnotebook@gmail.com

Facebook: Belle's Notebook
IG: Belle's Notebook

What resources do you currently have that will help you
achieve your goal?

_____

_____

_____

What resources do you need in order to achieve your goal?

_____

_____

_____

When you reach your balance goal you will be...

_____

_____

_____

What are your next steps towards your balance goals?
List three steps that you will take.

_____

_____

_____

_____

CHAPTER TWO

Self Care

I will be honest; in my twenties, I had no concept of self-care. I was laser focused on obtaining my degrees. I often was unemployed during this process and had limited money for what I believed were luxuries. I had this idea that self-care included spa treatments that I could not afford at the time. I made a choice to sacrifice this as I went through school and this was tough. It is no secret that I love spas. I love the atmosphere. I love getting series. They are my hideaway. I also have a lot of friends that own local spas. While financially I had to sacrifice this activity for a period of time, I did not realize at the time that self-care did not have to cost a lot of money.

During my college days, I never gave myself a break. While I was not employed full time during most of my college journey, I always had a lot of tasks to complete. This included homework, internships, research projects (not assigned for class), or babysitting. I often had to work for free and my motivation was building a curriculum vitae (CV). I can tell you that it eventually paid off. I reached my goal, but it cost me parts of myself.

I justified the lack of self-care by telling myself that it was for a good reason, that it would pay off in a few years, and that life will be easier when I finish. Now looking back, I realize how flawed my reasoning was. I still agree that it was for a great reason and the work paid off. One way it paid off was when I was hired as a full-time professor before my 30th birthday. The payoff in a few years, well, that all depends on how you look at it. Did I achieve my goal? Yes. Am I happy I did it? Of course. Did I hurt myself in the process? Yes. I missed out on parts of my 20s that I will never get back. I also let my health and weight suffer. I gained over forty pounds in my graduate school years and I was unhealthy. I also got a cold after every semester. To my last point about life getting easier after I finished. Well, life will always throw a curve ball. I was flawed to think life would be overall easier. There are certain parts of my life that are very nice due to my work (flexible schedule, opportunity to go to conferences all over the world) but my degrees do not stop the unpleasant things in life (divorce, sickness, financial stress). Life will continue to happen and that is simply a beautiful thing.

I was consistent with two things for self-care at this time - getting a haircut and getting facials. While it may seem silly, my hair was always something I made sure to take care of. Facials also seemed necessary. When I was a teen, I had acne all over my face and nothing seemed to cure it. I had tried multiple treatments but they were unsuccessful. My next step was to take strong medication. I was not a fan. I did not want to introduce the medication into my body for an acne problem. I did not know what else to try. My friend suggested I get a facial for my acne. I tried it and it was the solution that I needed!

After my first experience, I began to get facials on a regular basis. I saw an improvement in my skin. My acne became less frequent and less severe. At first, I would get a facial with the change of the season since this was all I could do at the time. Now, my facials have increased to monthly.

I continued to get facials throughout my twenties. This seemingly luxurious treatment was helping my skin, and I wanted to take care of my skin at a young age. I saw other positive benefits of the facials. My skin was clear, I saw anti-aging benefits, and the process was relaxing. I felt I was being proactive and this also made me feel good.

10

After finishing college, my self care routine has changed. I have to admit it took some time, and it is still a work in progress. However, I am getting better at finding time for myself and saying no to things (I used to say yes to everything because I thought I could do it all). This has significantly shifted my experience.

Another part of self-care that I am getting really good at is asking for help. At first, this took a lot of reminders from Peter. He would always ask me why I did not ask him for help. Honestly, it was because I was so used to having to do things by myself. This took a while, but I am at a point now where I realize the strength of teams and partnerships. I embrace it now versus looking at asking for help as a failure. This has been a radical shift in my own thinking.

Regardless of where you are in life at the moment, never neglect self-care. If my journey tells you anything, it is that this neglect has nothing but unpleasant consequences. Find the ways that you can take care of yourself and that make you happy. Simply put, self-care will look differently for everyone so find what works best for you.

Self Care

TIPS & TRICKS

Ask for help

WHETHER IT IS FROM YOUR PARTNER OR COLLEAGUES DO NOT FEEL LIKE YOU HAVE TO DO EVERYTHING ALONE!

Let someone assist you. This is especially true if they have strengths other than yours. Not only will you not be overwhelmed, but the outcome may be much better.

find what works for you

SELF-CARE WILL LOOK DIFFERENTLY TO EVERYONE

Sometimes, it is simply sitting in a quiet space for a few moments. In other cases, it will be buying something that you have always wanted. Whatever it is, do it and do it often.

Self care does not have to cost money

IT CAN BE A WALK IN THE PARK OR SPENDING SOME TIME WITH FAMILY AND FRIENDS.

Do not neglect the self-care because you believe it will be expensive or unaffordable.

WORKSHEET

Feel free to answer the questions in a way you feel comfortable (ex. writing, drawing). *Get creative!*

. . . .

Rest and self-care are so important. When you take time to replenish your spirit, it allows you to serve others from the overflow. You cannot serve from an empty vessel
- Eleanor Brown

. . . .

What is your goal for self-care?
(ex. monthly massage, quiet time)

_____

_____

_____

Why is this important to you?

_____

_____

_____

How close are you to achieving your self care goals?

_____

_____

_____

What resources do you currently have to achieve your goal?

_____

_____

_____

What resources do you need in order to achieve your goal?

_____

_____

_____

When you reach your self care goal you will be...

_____

_____

_____

What are your next steps towards your self care goals?
List three steps that you will take.

_____

_____

_____

_____

CHAPTER THREE

Education

My journey into education started early. As a child, I was always curious and learning. I loved to read books. One of my earliest memories was shopping at Caldor with my father for books. My personal favorite was the *Bernstein Bears*. He never said no to buying books and due to that I had quite an impressive collection of children's books.

I was also writing a lot. I used to have several notebooks that I filled with stories while sitting in the waiting rooms for doctor and dentist appointments. I wish I could tell you what I wrote in the notebooks, but I have no memory of the stories that I wrote in the notebooks.

My elementary school contributed to my love of writing. There was a publishing room in my elementary school filled with typewriters, book covers, and volunteers. When we wrote stories in class that were complete the teacher would send us to the publishing room. There we would get the chance to pick a book cover and spine. The volunteers would type up our stories and bind them together. Once this process was complete, usually a few days later, we would receive our books in class. I loved getting my book back and seeing the complete package. Then the next step would begin - we got to illustrate our creations! There were also a few school days where we could display our work to the entire school. This process opened my young mind to possibilities of writing and publishing a book. This early introduction shaped a large part of my educational future.

My middle and high school years were filled with the typical uncertainty teenagers face. I was focused on making friends and finding my place in life. I was also a bit lost because I was truly interested in academics. I was great with History and English. I struggled with Math and Sciences. It was also not the cool thing to actually like school. I wanted to fit in with my friends and be accepted. I focused on that part of my life through high school.

As the end of high school came near, I had to make the same decision my peers were going to make. I had to apply to college. I went through the SATs. I should also note that I am a bad test taker. While I was a strong A and B student, tests always gave me anxiety. When I took the SATs, I failed them. Like literally failed the SATs. I took the exam twice and I failed both times. I did not think much of it, simply that I was bad at tests, until I received letters back from the colleges I applied to.

I did not have many options when I received my letters back from colleges. My SATs did not help me. I was not sure what I was going to do. A month after I received my rejection from the University of Connecticut, I received a second letter in the mail. It was an acceptance to a regional campus. I was excited and confused. What had changed their mind?

I went to school the next day and showed my guidance counselor the letter. She was thrilled and then she solved my mystery. She was an adjunct at the regional campus. When she heard of my rejection from the school, she sent letters and advocated for my acceptance. I was a strong student and I should not be defined by my test score. The admissions teams saw it the same way and changed their mind. I was thrilled! My future looked bright again. I graduated high school with a decent grade point average and with many lifelong friends.

I enrolled in college and fell in love with academics again. I had several ideas for majors and was unsure of what to study. I was curious about social sciences and wanted to use my education to help people. I quickly found that I was good at Sociology and pursued it as a major. I graduated with a bachelor's with Sociology and Communications.

I went straight to work in a group home after graduation. I still was unsure of what industry I wanted to go into. I was happy to have a full-time job even though I was not making a lot of money. I quickly realized that something was missing from my life and that was school. I applied to a graduate program in Social Work. I was quickly rejected from that program. I felt as though I had failed. All I wanted was to pursue a degree and I was not good enough (or so I felt that way!). I did not know what to do so, I focused on work.

I spent two years working in a group home. I learned a lot, but I was truly unhappy in that role. I wanted to help people, but this did not feel like it was right for me. I only left the job after my grandmother died. I had no plan and I struggled for a year.

On the first anniversary of my grandmother's passing, I was extremely sad and cried the whole day. When I woke up the next morning, I realized she would be so angry with me. I was wasting my life on sadness. I was not pursing a job or a degree. This was not the life she wanted from me. She was a survivor of World War II. She struggled financially her entire adult life. I was throwing my life away because I was sad. This was a wakeup call for me. I called the Admissions Department at Central Connecticut State University and scheduled an appointment. The Admissions Representative guided me to their Counseling program. I would achieve my goal of helping people and gain a clinical background in the field.

I took one class before I officially applied to the program. I fell in love. I felt like I was growing again. The class was interesting. My classmates were wonderful people. I wanted to be accepted into the program.

I applied and was accepted a few months later! I was thrilled again. My life felt like it was getting back on track. Due to the nature of the program, I had to take classes during the day. It was hard to find a full-time job. I struggled financially during the duration of the program but I loved being in school. I learned so much and I felt as though I was growing as a person.

During my time in my master's program, I flourished. I got to have many new experiences. I chaired an international conference at the college focused on my Polish roots. I got to meet politicians from both Poland and the United States. This reminded me of my book publishing in elementary school, where the world was open to me and I could accomplish anything.

Towards the end of my master's program, I felt as though I was not finished. I applied to and was accepted into my doctoral program. I did not have a break between programs. I started the doctoral program the week I finished my master's program. It was tiring, but I would not have it any other way.

My doctoral program filled my life for the next four years. It was still difficult to find employment due to the economy and my class schedule. I was broke but happy. I was in a program that made sense to me, and I felt like I was good at it. I learned to be an awesome researcher. I also got an opportunity to teach a class at a regional campus of the University of Connecticut. It was focused on the Polish experience in America. This class gave me creative control and married my international conference experience. This launched my teaching career.

I began my teaching career as an adjunct. I began teaching entry level courses at the college level. I was an adjunct for a year before I was offered the full-time position. I began working full time and it finally felt as though things were falling into place!

As I began my full-time position, I still needed to finish my doctorate. It still took me about a year and a half to get my degree. Life was a bit hectic with a full-time job, the demanding work of a dissertation, and moving in with my new boyfriend. It took a lot, but I would not change this time in my life for anything.

Even when I received my degree, I kept learning. I signed up for training in a new teaching method. I began to apply it to my work and redesigned courses. I kept doing research. I never allowed graduation to stop me from learning. In fact, it opened up my time to learn new things.

While I decided to pursue multiple college degrees, I was still learning from all parts of my life. I was learning from friends. I was learning from experiences. I was learning from the challenges I faced. This all built character. It showed me what I could accomplish even when I was faced with obstacles. The most important lesson that I learned from pursing my degrees is that I am capable. What better lesson to learn?

Education

TIPS & TRICKS

follow your Passion

SPENDING MULTIPLE YEARS IN A FORMAL EDUCATION SETTING CAN BE A DIFFICULT TASK.

Pursuing a degree requires a lot of sacrifice especially your time. If you are going to spend your life working on something, it better be something you love.

Encourage people to be Curious

LEARNING IS A LIFELONG PROCESS

It happens both in and out of the classroom. Always be curious about the world around you and to learn more about it.

Advocate for others

IF MY GUIDANCE COUNSELOR DID NOT ADVOCATE FOR ME, MY LIFE MIGHT BE VERY DIFFERENT RIGHT NOW.

She saw something in me and wanted me to become more. I did. I repaid her by pursuing my degrees. Advocate for others because you never know how you may change someone's life.

WORKSHEET

Feel free to answer the questions in a way you feel comfortable (ex. writing, drawing). *Get creative!*

. . . .

The beautiful thing about learning
is nobody can take it away from you.
- B.B. King

. . . .

What is your goal in education?
(ex. to learn more, get a degree, for a promotion)

_____

_____

_____

Why is this important to you?

_____

_____

_____

How close are you to achieving your goals in education?

_____

_____

_____

What resources do you currently have to achieve your goal?

_____

_____

_____

What resources do you need in order to achieve your goal?

_____

_____

_____

When you reach your education goal you will be...

_____

_____

_____

What are your next steps towards your education goals?
List three steps that you will take.

_____

_____

_____

_____

CHAPTER FOUR

Fitness

In society today, there is a strong focus on fitness. There always seems to be a new gym, diet, exercise routine, or fast solution that continues to flood the market. It can be overwhelming. I catch myself asking, "which diet is right for me? What exercises should I do to achieve my goals? How do I fit this in to my already tight schedule?"

My own journey with physical fitness has been one of stops and starts. As a child, I was very athletic. I took dance lessons for nine years in tap, ballet, and jazz. I played basketball. I ran around with my cousins. I did not have to think about physical fitness because it was just a part of my daily life.

As I came into my teen years, I slowly started letting going of some activities. I was more focused on friends at that time and then myself. I stopped playing basketball on a team. Then I quit dance. Then college happened.

I was a commuting student in college. I attended a regional campus for two years and then went to the main branch of the University of Connecticut. This was a 45-minute commute daily. I was working part time at a dermatologist's office and balancing a full college course load. I was not thinking about the gym. I also experienced a lot of life changes during my college years. This included a break up with my high school boyfriend and being a caregiver to my grandmother. My focus remained on other people in my life.

When I graduated from college, I was focused on getting into graduate school and getting a full time job. I got a full time job in the human services field but did not get into graduate school. My break from school lasted almost three years. I was working full time and adjusting to a new life. I attempted some graduate courses at the local college and was not doing so well. That semester my grandmother passed away. She passed away on the last night of classes and I did poorly on the final a week after her funeral. I thought my graduate school opportunities were never going to happen.

I quit my job two weeks after she passed away. I did not know what I wanted to do and I did not have a plan. I struggled that year. I did not care. I went another year without graduate school because I was scared of being rejected.

The turning point came on the first anniversary of my grandmothers passing. It was the first moment, in a long time, where I decided to turn my life around. I realized she would be so upset with me because I was letting my life go nowhere. I made choices that brought my life to a standstill. She would not want that for me.

I started the process of getting into graduate school. I went to a different program. I spoke to faculty members there. I took a class. It took six months, but I got into the program. I was excited, but the program schedule made it hard to work. I would struggle with work throughout the program.

A few months before graduation, I had this feeling that I was not done with my education. I was also mentored into applying to a doctoral program. I applied and got in. I was running scared. I wanted to keep the momentum going because of my past rejection with school. I graduated with my master's degree and started my doctoral program a month later.

My doctoral program took up the next four years of my life. I was able to go back to work full time because the program was designed to accommodate that. Halfway through my program, the opportunity to train at a local gym presented itself. I could only commit to one day a week due to time and financial restraints, but I figured something was better than nothing.

I trained for about a year. I had to quit because I moved away and needed to focus on my dissertation. This was the right move for me to finish school but not physically. I would not make it back to the gym for another three years.

In that three-year break, there was no consistent exercise routine. I only did some activities once in a while like hiking, yoga, or bike riding. I felt as though I did not have enough time and the cost was too high. It was the first time in my life that I tried different diets. That was an interesting experience!

I never really saw true results from the different diets that I tried. I also noticed a consistent weight gain every year when I went to annual check ups. I would speak to my physicians and express my concern. Their response was consistent-you are stressed, go get some rest, and you look fine.

That is the thing; I always looked fine, but I was not happy about where I was. I did not feel great either. I had some pains in my legs that started. I felt sluggish. I did not want to continue on this path.

I finally decided it was time to make a change. I began working with a trainer in one on one sessions. This made all the difference. I felt as though I could focus on the specific areas that I wanted to focus on and also reach my individual goals.

So, what is the point in telling you my fitness story by weaving in my educational journey? It was that I spent fifteen years putting something or someone else first. I always had a reason as to why I did not go to the gym or work with a trainer. This included the cost of it, not having enough time, being tired, and there always seemed to be something more important to do. My story also includes all of the factors that could influence the success of training. It is not just about going to the gym; it is also about the outside influences that can hurt or help your progress.

The reality was that I was putting myself last. I was not taking care of myself in the physical form. This was not about a number on a scale or a dress size. This was about reaching a goal I had for myself. Signing up for training was an act of putting myself first and self love.

As you think about your own fitness journey, think about all the factors that go into a fitness routine. Do not be another person that signs up to the gym and quickly forgets about the membership. Also, find the appropriate method that works for you. Make the appropriate changes that make sense for your life and commit.

Fitness

TIPS & TRICKS

find the right Routine

THERE ARE SO MANY DIETS, METHODS, AND CLASSES OUT THERE

Do some research and find which one works the best for you. Know and understand your body. Consult with experts (trainers, nutritionists, and physicians) about what makes the most sense for your body.

Commit

MAKE THE COMMITMENT

Do not sign up for the gym just because it is a New Year's resolution or because your friends pressured you into it. If you do not commit, that gym membership will quickly turn into a direct debit from your bank account that you forget about. Do not waste your money and time. Both are important resources.

Know your Purpose

FIGURE OUT YOUR REASON FOR GOING TO THE GYM

It is easier to commit and fight through all the challenges when you know what your purpose is. Set goals. Meet them. Set new goals.

WORKSHEET

Feel free to answer the questions in a way you feel comfortable (ex. writing, drawing). *Get creative!*

. . . .

You must expect great things of yourself
before you can do them.
- Michael Jordan

. . . .

What is your fitness goal?
(ex. lose weight, tone, feel better)

_____

_____

_____

Why is this important to you?

_____

_____

_____

How close are you to achieving your fitness goals?

_____

_____

_____

What resources do you currently have to achieve your goal?

_____

_____

_____

What resources do you need in order to achieve your goal?

_____

_____

_____

When you reach your fitness goal you will be...

_____

_____

_____

What are your next steps towards your fitness goals?
List three steps that you will take.

_____

_____

_____

_____

CHAPTER FIVE

Food

Eating is essential to life. It is one of the basic needs for survival. Along with the basic need for survival, food is also a celebration. It brings families together for a meal. It is the cornerstone of large gatherings. It highlights cultural variation. It can also be comforting and bring up favorite memories. The best cooking also comes from the heart.

As a society, we have an interesting relationship with food. I often hear people say they do not have time to cook and opt for quick meals. In a weight loss journey, diets that limit food calories are often the first choice. My job is to write about having a healthy relationship with food. A relationship with foods needs to feed your soul but also your body. It is a relationship that is overwhelmingly positive and not negative.

I am no chef, but I am a cook. Some of my earliest memories include helping my grandmother in the kitchen. I loved being able to help her and at the same time, learn something new. One thing my grandmother focused on is teaching me how to make pierogi.

From the moment I was old enough to watch a pot of water boil, I was the lead supervisor of cooking the pierogi. While I waited for my new job to begin, I would watch my grandmother make the pierogi out of flour, butter, eggs, and all the other ingredients. As a child, I watched in amazement how she turned things (the individual ingredients) into a delicious meal. She would sit there for hours because she only made them a few times a year and always made a lot of them at one time! When it was time to cook the pierogi, I felt like I was contributing to the process. I became an expert on when to take them out of the water and how to separate them on the plate (individually and putting butter on right away so they do not stick together).

As I grew up, she taught me different parts of the process. I soon learned how to make the dough and roll it out to the correct consistency. I learned how much filling to place into the small circles we made from a cookie cutter (just enough so you can still pinch both sides). I learned how to make the different fillings (however, she never taught me her cabbage recipe. I think she did that on purpose). I became a pierogi expert as a teenager.

When I hit my teen years, the days she called me for help with making pierogi seemed like an inconvenience. It was an all-day process and I wanted to sleep in! I did not want to stand over pots and pans all day to make one dish. I had friends to hang out with! She still made me help. After all, making pierogi is a team task (especially in the amounts that she made). Today, I can say I am grateful for all of the practice.

The week before my grandmother passed away, she made a lot of pierogi. She spent two days making them. The process almost spilled over into a third day. I thought this was strange because she typically made them on a weekend and this time her process started on Monday. She got sick that Saturday and passed away the next Monday.

While she never said it and I cannot prove it, I feel as though she was making the pierogi to make sure I had something to eat. This is when I realized food is an act of love. The process of cooking and feeding someone is a true gesture of love. It is caring for someone and making sure their basic needs are met.

Today, I am still an expert in making pierogi (the only cooking title I will ever give myself). I can say that because I had years of training as an apprentice to my grandmother. I still hold on to her traditional recipe. When I make them, I am reminded of the time that I spent making them with her. It is also fulfilling to make something people enjoy eating.

Cooking also does not have to be viewed as a chore. In today's fast paced society, you may not have a full day to make pierogi. However, there are plenty of quick recipes that can be prepared after a long day. There are also plenty of life hacks to help make a quick and healthy meal on a daily basis. This includes prepared salad mixes, quick recipes, and meal prepping in advance.

I have learned a lot in preparing not only pierogi but also with the meals I prepare to feed my family. I find cooking to be fun because it is a chance to experiment with new things. In addition to being a way to take care of my family and friends, I also find it to be a method of self-expression. I also like the learning process and developing my skills.

I mentioned earlier that I am not a trained chef but a cook. I am also not a nutrition expert, rather a person who has changed my eating patterns to feed my body and as I began weight training. In that experience, I have also learned a few things. The most important of which is to eat real food.

There are plenty of diets, diet hacks, and supplements that hold a lot of promises. The two questions that I would ask is "does it feed your body? Does it feed your soul?" If the answer is no, do not pursue it further. It is also not a good idea to not feed your body. It needs the nutrients to keep your body healthy and going. This is all necessary to have a healthy relationship with food.

Also, feed your body the food that it likes and wants. Figure out what your body needs and eat towards those needs. For example, I have never been a great fan of meat (I am not vegetarian, but I do not crave meat as much as other foods). Due to that, I eat more fish and vegetables. While I need the protein, meat sources may not work best for my body.

At any point in your cooking and food journey, remember that food should be enjoyed. Whether it is changing your diet for weight loss or to eat healthier, find the options that make you happy. If you do not enjoy it, you will not stick with it. Always remember to do what you love, even when it comes to food.

Food

TIPS & TRICKS

Meal Prep

**WHEN YOU HAVE SOME FREE TIME,
PREP MULTIPLE MEALS IN ADVANCE.**

This will save time during busier days of your week. Some meals can be in the refrigerator for a few days while others can be frozen and then reheated prior to eating. This will help by having meals ready and avoiding last minute decisions.

Eat for your body

KNOW WHAT YOUR BODY NEEDS.

If you prefer certain foods over others, eat the foods you prefer. Also, if there are any allergies or food sensitivities, make sure you eat towards that type of diet.

Do not be afraid to try new things

TRY NEW THINGS IN FOODS

This can be through eating out or cooking new things. Do not be afraid to try new combinations because you never know if you will find a new meal you will love.

WORKSHEET

Feel free to answer the questions in a way you feel
comfortable (ex. writing, drawing). *Get creative!*

. . . .

Food is our common ground,
a universal experience.
- James Beard

. . . .

What is your goal with food?
(ex. try new things, weight loss, eat healthier)

_____

_____

_____

Why is this important to you?

_____

_____

_____

How close are you to achieving your food goals?

_____

_____

_____

What resources do you currently have to achieve your goal?

_____

_____

_____

What resources do you need in order to achieve your goal?

_____

_____

_____

When you reach your food goal you will be...

_____

_____

_____

What are your next steps towards your food goals?
List three steps that you will take.

_____

_____

_____

_____

CHAPTER SIX

Finances

I have to admit; this is a topic that I have the least experience with. In reality, I have made plenty of financial mistakes in my twenties and graduate school years. The best way I can talk to you about financial health is to tell you what not to do.

Let me put it into perspective. At the end of high school and throughout college I worked at a dermatologist's office. I left the job before I finished college because I had to commute to campus and my class schedule did not fit the job schedule. I graduated college in December 2007. Probably the worst time in recent history to start out in the workforce. As the market crashed in 2008, so did my job and salary opportunities.

My first job out of college was a good beginning but I was also significantly underpaid. I was grateful for the job, but I was making significantly less than my peers. At first, my plan was to work for a bit and get into graduate school. I figured this would open me up to other opportunities. When I did not get into my graduate program I quickly became stuck and did not know how to move forward.

I made a mistake when my grandmother passed away. This is when I made the quick decision to leave my job. I figured this was a way to move ahead with my life. The problem was I did not have a job lined up and I did not look for one.

I was not thinking straight and I made a big decision with little information.

I spent that next year significantly underemployed. I lost my way. I was in my mid-twenties and going nowhere with my life. I did not know which direction to go in. I went back into human services temporarily. This only confirmed that I did not want to be in the field in the long run. I left my job pretty quickly. I still had no plan.

After being unemployed for a bit, I decided to switch gears completely. I went to work as a bank teller. It was a new field to me. I figured it would be a job that brought some type of income while I figured my life out. Here, I was a college graduate unsure of herself and working in a field that I knew very little about. I felt like a failure. I felt like I failed myself not because I was working as a teller, but because I was not doing what I had set out to do in college. I started to do some research about graduate school.

Slowly but surely, my life began to change. The position helped me to refocus my life. I applied and got into graduate school. I began classes and experienced some success with school. I applied for a job at a local college. I was offered the position and left my teller job to work for the college. However, this success was short lived. The new position interrupted my class schedule. I had to make a choice; remain employed full time or pursue my master's degree. I chose my master's degree.

Since I left the bank on good terms, I went back to being a teller for the summer. It allowed me to continue my studies with some income. After the summer was over, my internships started which kept me away from working again.

I never wanted to have short stints at jobs, but I ran into situations where I needed to make a choice. There never seemed to be an option that combined my student needs and my financial needs. This time in my life made me fall significantly financially behind.

Once I earned my master's degree, I went straight into my doctorate. During the first two years of that program, I only worked as a research assistant. These positions are usually a few months, temporary, and pay a set stipend (not an hourly wage). My first break into teaching came when I was offered an adjunct position at a college that I wanted to work at for a few years. I was out of college for seven years and felt as though it was my first real break!

An adjunct is a part time worker at the college level. I was still not making the money I needed, but I was finally in a career I wanted to be in. On the days that I was not on campus, I was taking care of my newborn nephew. I was certainly busy between work, taking care of a newborn, and continuing my doctoral work.

After a year of working as an adjunct, I was offered the full time position at the college. I was happy to accept. I felt as though all my years of hard work and sacrifice were paying off. I was not yet thirty and I had earned the title of Assistant Professor. I was ecstatic.

I have remained employed at the same institution since the job offer. I have grown as a professional and as an individual in that role. It took a long time, but I found stability for the first time since I graduated college. This gave me some peace in my life and allowed me to move on to other things in my life.

As I mentioned earlier, I made plenty of financial mistakes. I left jobs before I should have due to emotions. I experienced periods of unemployment. I had difficulties in obtaining full time positions. I also had to do it all on my own.

I wished I had better financial sense. I wished there was more money in my bank account. I admit that I sometimes wondered if I should have made different choices. The thing is I figured it all out.

Those moments are temporary as I would never truly change anything that I experienced. This period of difficulty showed me that I am stronger than I realized, taught me more about money than I would have learned if I was always financially comfortable, and strengthened my character. I can always find a way to make more money, but I could not learn these life lessons in any other way.

Finances

TIPS & TRICKS

Ask the Expert

WHEN IT COMES TO FINANCIAL DECISIONS, ASK THE EXPERTS.

They are the best option to inquire about investments, financial plans, or financial products that may help you reach your goals.

Weigh your options

WHEN MAKING LIFE CHOICES THAT INFLUENCE YOUR FINANCIAL GOALS, LOOK AT ALL OF YOUR OPTIONS.

Make a pro and con list. See what option makes the most financial sense. If necessary, consult with a financial expert.

Live your life

WHILE IT IS IMPORTANT TO SAVE AND MAKE GOOD FINANCIAL DECISIONS, DO NOT LET IT STOP YOU FROM LIVING YOUR LIFE.

Allow yourself some rewards. Do not wait until retirement to take a big trip or to experience something you have always wanted to. Keep your life in balance.

WORKSHEET

Feel free to answer the questions in a way you feel
comfortable (ex. writing, drawing). *Get creative!*

. . . .

Money is a guarantee that we may have what we want in the future.
Though we need nothing at the moment it insures the possibility of
satisfying a new desire when it arises.
- Aristotle

. . . .

What is your financial goal?
(ex. earn more, save more, build wealth)

_____

_____

_____

Why is this important to you?

_____

_____

_____

How close are you to achieving your financial goals?

_____

_____

_____

What resources do you currently have to achieve your goal?

_____

_____

_____

What resources do you need in order to achieve your goal?

_____

_____

_____

When you reach your financial goal you will be...

_____

_____

_____

What are your next steps towards your financial goals?
List three steps that you will take.

_____

_____

_____

_____

Relationship
with Others

The next chapters focus on
your relationship with other people.

CHAPTER SEVEN

Family

My family of origin is a large and complex group of people. I have many aunts, uncles, cousins, second cousins, and relatives through marriage. Many of them are immigrants from Poland. They reside in the United States and in Poland. At this point, many of my cousins have their own children which adds to the family dynamic.

I cannot discuss my family dynamic without including the history of immigration from Poland to the United States. Many of my family members were originally born there and came to the United States at some point in their lives. This includes family members of all ages. This includes my husband who was fifteen when he arrived in Connecticut from Krosno, Poland.

Growing up in a large immigrant family leads to a number of important lessons. The first is understanding history (both familial and world history). Many of my family members experienced World War II in Poland. They have varied experiences and most were in their middle school years during the war. When the war ended, they did not forget their experiences and carried their traumas into their adult lives. As a child, I heard bits and pieces about the war (based on what they felt comfortable sharing). By the time I got to high school and the subject came up in history, I had a wealth of knowledge based on first-hand accounts to share with my class. This also gave me a new perspective of my life in the United States.

The next topic of consideration in this type of family dynamic is language. I grew up speaking Polish before I spoke English (my caregivers only spoke Polish to me). I learned English in pre-school. When I got to second grade in my American school, my parents signed me up for Polish school on Saturday mornings. There we learned the Polish language, history, and geography. I completed the school when I was in eighth grade in my American school. I still speak Polish (still working on grammar) but it has become a part of my daily life and identity.

Lastly, there are plenty of cultural norms and traditions that may be different from mainstream society. Our Christmas traditions are a bit different (Christmas Eve is the bigger holiday). Most family vacations are spent going back to Poland to visit relatives still living there. This may even guide who you become when you grow up.

As I was growing up, I realized that I was different. I loved my family, the culture, and traditions, but I was always curious of more. I always felt as though the world was bigger than my hometown and I wanted to experience it. I wanted to travel. I wanted to study and learn. I wanted to meet new people. I was also more interested in school while my peers were getting married and beginning families.

At first, this idea of being different hurt me. I wanted to fit in and be accepted by my peers. As time went on, I realized that I was heading in a different path. I had my own journey to pursue and that was ok. This created a divide in some relationships and more hurt. I wished that my family members supported me. Some did, while others did not. I quickly learned that they did not understand my journey or how to support me on it.

This experience helped me to create a family of my choice. It was not my intention to do so; I was simply making and looking for friends who were on a similar path that I was on. They became my mentors, supporters, and shoulders to lean on during tough times. My family of choice is filled with peoples from diverse backgrounds. This includes age, cultural background, educational status, religion, race, and ethnicity. I have learned a lot from each individual and they continue to shape me.

Another member of my family of choice includes my husband. We chose each other when we were dating and made the decision to get married together. There was no official proposal! More on that in the next book. We often hear from people that we got lucky to find each other. While luck may have played a part in our initial meeting, the rest was our choice. We chose the path we are on right now and to work on our relationship every day.

I have to say that I am grateful for both of my families. Each family gave me a unique experience and significantly influenced who I am today. My family of origin taught me how to form relationships, how to be supportive, and my values. They taught me the value of history, the importance of language, and how to be kind. My family of choice positively pushed me in my self-development. They helped me to dream and reach further in my life. As a result, I have had some amazing opportunities and experiences including seeing new places, trying new things, and reaching a new professional level.

Another major life lesson I learned from both families is that families change. These changes will be due to people entering your life or leaving your life. The dynamic of your family will change due to marriage, new births, adoptions, divorce, and when people pass away. This will lead to some of the best and worst moments of your life. Let it all happen. It will shape you into the person that you are becoming.

This will also lead to your roles and responsibilities changing. One day ,you are a child and sibling and the next, you are the parent. The people that you include in your family will also change. That is ok. The change in dynamic will help you grow as an individual.

Family

TIPS & TRICKS

Know your family of origin

**GET TO KNOW YOUR FAMILY ON
A DIFFERENT LEVEL.**

Get to know your family history. Learn about
your culture of origin. Connect with your
family members on a deeper level (getting
to know their goals and dreams). It may
strengthen a relationship going forward.

find your family of choice

I AM A BIG FAN OF EXPERIENCE.

Your family of choice will give you new
experiences and insights that are different
from your family of origin. They may also be
able to support you in different ways such as
your professional career.

Be ok with change

YOUR ROLE IN YOUR FAMILY WILL CHANGE.

That is inevitable. Your relationships will change.
It is scary, but also an opportunity to grow as
an individual.

WORKSHEET

Feel free to answer the questions in a way you feel comfortable (ex. writing, drawing). *Get creative!*

. . . .

Other things may change us,
but we start and end with the family.
- Anthony Brandt

. . . .

What is your family goal?
(ex. get married, stay single, have children)

_____

_____

_____

Why is this important to you?

_____

_____

_____

How close are you to achieving your family goals?

_____

_____

_____

What resources do you currently have to achieve your goal?

_____

_____

_____

What resources do you need in order to achieve your goal?

_____

_____

_____

When you reach your family goal you will be...

_____

_____

_____

What are your next steps towards your family goals?
List three steps that you will take.

_____

_____

_____

_____

CHAPTER EIGHT

Friendships

Friendships are an instrumental part of life. We first make friends as children in school and on the playground. As we get older our friendships evolve. Over the course of a lifetime, we make new friends, lose friends, and redefine friendships. The purpose of friendship also changes.

As a child I was very active and athletic. I was involved in dance class for about a decade. I played basketball. I took music lessons. I attended Polish Saturday school. I had plenty of ways to make friends in the different aspects of my life.

Growing up, I had the same group of friends. We met in Polish school, in dance class, or through family friends. We would hang out to watch movies or play games. As we grew into teenagers, we attended different schools but still remained friends. Our activities evolved into typical teenager interests including parties, boys, and shopping.

We all graduated high school around the same time (within a year or two of each other). We went off to college. Some chose a four-year college while others went to a community college. We all have very different career aspirations. Some members of the group knew exactly what they wanted to do, went to school for it, and quickly began working in their field. Some members knew they were going to college but unsure of what they waned to do. They went to college, got a degree, and went to work. I wanted to keep going to school. I was the outlier.

This is the time that I saw rifts in our friendships. I wanted to continue on to school. They were moving on to a different part of their lives. They were getting their first jobs, getting married, and buying houses. I was wondering how to pay tuition for graduate school. There were times where I worried about affording certain things that they could such as bachelorette party weekends or even furniture for my first apartment. We were in very different places in our lives.

I would remain friendly with this group of friends, but the rift continued to get bigger. I was naive enough to think that it only began to happen in our twenties. If I wanted to be honest, the differences were already there. I was just late to notice. Over time, the invitations stopped coming. I also had to decline some invitations. We simply grew apart.

At the same time that I was experiencing differences with my childhood friends, I was making new friendships in graduate school. This new chapter of my life exposed me to new people, a new schedule, and a new purpose. I made several new friendships. Some friendships were temporary. Some of my new friends turned into my colleagues. I was moving in a new direction and my new friends understood my life. They knew the pressures of graduate school, of my academic career, and the stress of completing a dissertation.

I reconnected with another group of friends from high school that I lost touch with. It was as if time did not pass. We picked right up where we left off. There were no hard feelings for missed weddings, family events, or grudges. There was just a genuine interest in starting anew.

I made new friends when I began working in my current job. They work in various departments across the institution. We bonded over a shared mission, likes, and interests. We also get to work on different projects together. It makes work even more fun when you get to work with your friends.

I also made friends with business owners including estheticians, makeup artists, and hair dressers. I am a very loyal customer when I find someone that I work well with. These friendships grew due to my repeat visits to their business. These friendships also provided me with a new perspective on business and their particular industry. I learned a lot about business, skincare, and hair care through our conversations. I felt as though I was growing through these friendships.

My relationship with Peter also opened me up to new friendships. He already had a circle of friends that I got the opportunity to meet and hang out with. We also developed new friendships as a couple. This typically happens as we make friends with the owners of our favorite business.

I can admit that I sometimes struggle with finding time for my friends as my career and business are continuing to grow. I also have a marriage that is very important to me. I sometimes feel guilty that I cannot give more time to my friends, that I miss texts, or have to reschedule dates. I try my best and I believe my friends know that. I also understand that they have similar issues in their lives. This kind of communication and understanding helps to maintain the friendships.

It seems the rule with friendships is they keep changing and evolving. This happens as you change and evolve as an individual. If you have the opportunity to maintain the same friendships since childhood, that is amazing but just make sure that the friendship grows with your individual growth. If your friendships grow apart, that is also fine. Take the lessons that you learned in those friendships, be grateful for each lesson, and apply them to your life or new friendships.

Friendships

TIPS & TRICKS

Communication

LIKE ANY RELATIONSHIP, COMMUNICATION WITH FRIENDS IS KEY.

Let them know what is going on in your life. Be honest when you cannot make an event.

Evaluate your friendships

ASK YOURSELF HOW YOU FEEL ABOUT A PARTICULAR FRIENDSHIP.

Does it make you feel good? Does it make you feel nervous? Does your friend understand if you cannot make it to certain events? When you get together, are there guilt trips or chats that feel like there has not been any gap in time? The answers to these questions will help guide your decisions about particular friendships.

Know when it is time to move on

AT TIMES, WE ALL MAY HAVE TO LEAVE FRIENDSHIPS BEHIND.

It is ok if you have outgrown your friendships and feel as though it is time to move in a different direction. Do not feel guilty. Allow yourself to move in the direction that is best for you.

Celebrate your friends anywhere

BE HAPPY FOR THEM IN THEIR SUCCESS.

Be there for them when they have a hard time. Celebrate their life choices even if they are different than yours. Support goes a long way in any type of relationship.

You can make friends anywhere

DO NOT LIMIT YOURSELF TO CERTAIN GROUPS OF FRIENDS.

Do not rule out the people you work with, business owners, or even friends of friends. You may be missing out on some great friends if you are not open to it.

WORKSHEET

Feel free to answer the questions in a way you feel comfortable (ex. writing, drawing). *Get creative!*

. . . .

A real friend is one who walks in
when the rest of the world walks out.
- Walter Winchell

. . . .

What are your friendship goals?
(ex. make new friends, maintain relationships)

_____

_____

_____

Why is this important to you?

_____

_____

_____

How close are you to achieving your friendship goals?

_____

_____

_____

What resources do you currently have to achieve your goal?

_____

_____

_____

What resources do you need in order to achieve your goal?

_____

_____

_____

When you reach your friendship goals you will be...

_____

_____

_____

What are your next steps towards your friendship goals?
List three steps that you will take.

_____

_____

_____

CHAPTER NINE

Romantic Relationships

In my early twenties, I thought that I would marry my high school boyfriend, have children, and have my life settled by the time I turned thirty.

Boy was I wrong!

I started dating my high school boyfriend when I was seventeen and the relationship lasted nearly five years. We went to proms together, attended parties, and supported one another during our respective high school graduations. He was my best friend. We were typical teenagers. It was all adorable.

After high school, I knew I was going to college, but he was not so sure. I commuted to the University of Connecticut and he eventually decided to attend college as well. It all seemed to be working out. Everyone thought we were going to get married after college and I began to believe it. However, I was not paying attention.

In some ways, we were great together and in others we were not. I have to admit that at this time in my life I did not really understand relationships at all. I did not understand communication, active listening skills, or conflict resolution. We were growing apart, and I did not realize until it was too late. He grew distant. He was hinting to me he was not happy. We were not working on our relationship. Then one day, he left.

Like, literally left.

He told me he needed a break from our relationship to figure out what he wanted. He wanted to remain friends and at first, we tried to make that work. He never wanted to talk about our relationship, and he never formally broke up with me. Even though I asked for a reason, he never gave me one. I told him I would be his friend, and I was naive enough to think this would work.

The thing is I did not love myself enough to demand more.

I deserved more from him in terms of communication and my friendship. I did not understand the value of my friendship and respect. I allowed myself to be treated poorly by someone I formerly loved. This continued on for a few years. I allowed him to play with my emotions because I thought things would change.

During this time, I remained single. I went on a few dates, but the dates did not result in relationships. I threw myself into school. It was the only thing I could rely on during this time in my life.

One night at a party, I finally made the change. We happened to be at the same Halloween party. To be clear here, we were only friends and I was trying to make the friendship work. I wanted to be cordial with him and not feel awkward if we ran into each other. I did not see a reason at the time to not restore the friendship.

At the party, I was introduced to his new friend. His friend began asking me questions to get to know me and my ex answered the questions for me. I took him on the side to have a conversation. He was still being vague and denying things. He also told me he was dating someone new. I also caught him in a lie. At that moment, I knew I was done with any kind of relationship with my ex. I turned around and walked away. He did not deserve any part of me, including my friendship. I was going to make the change in relationship and take my friendship away. I deserved someone who treated me with respect and valued my friendship. We have not spoken since.

This act opened me up to other relationships. When I walked away, I was ready to move on. My next relationship was with someone who had similar academic interests. It seemed like the way to go. He was someone who understood the process of obtaining multiple degrees and working in academia. I thought it was the way to make a relationship work, through having someone understand my work interests.

Wrong again.

Just because someone understood my job did not mean we were on the same page with everything else. He was ready to move on, get married, and start a family. I was only ready to start a doctoral program. He had completed all of his academic work. I had just been accepted into my program and I needed to see if I could successfully complete it. He also lived in a different state. It only made sense for me to move. I was not ready to make that step.

We quickly realized that things would not work out. We spoke about it and made a joint decision. We decided to remain friends and we still are!

Yes, it is possible! You can be friends with an ex!

He has moved on and created a beautiful family. We chat on occasion to check in, wish each other happy holidays, and I have even asked him for work related advice. His friendship has been a valuable contribution to my life and I am grateful for it.

He moved on and I focused on school.

I figured I was going to spend my life alone. My relationships did not work out and the men in my life were able to move on quickly. I was focused on school and becoming a professor. I figured that was my purpose in life and I slowly became comfortable with that idea.

I threw myself back into my schoolwork. It was safe. It was challenging. It was less emotionally draining than relationships that did not work out. I swore off relationships.

Then the cute IT guy happened.

I was hired as a part time instructor at my current institution at the end of August, 2014. During my orientation, I was taken to the IT office to take my ID photo. The person leading my orientation informed me that one of the IT guys was Polish and that he might be in the office. Sure enough, he was there!

I walked in and the only person in the office was Piotr (Peter). I said hello to him in Polish and he was totally thrown off because it was unexpected for him. I though he was cute but I was very awkward. I talked a lot, he took the photo, gave me my ID, and I ran out of the office. This is how I met my husband.

Over the next few months, I would periodically see him in the hallway or in the staff lounge. We would chat and we got to know each other. We developed a friendship, but there were no romantic indications. Then came May, 2015.

We began talking a little more. He asked for my phone number. We tried to meet up outside of work but something always got in our way. He finally asked me out to lunch and we were able to meet up!

We met for sushi. I thought it was going to be a nice lunch with a friend and that I would be home by early evening to work on my research project. I was wrong again. Our sushi date lasted seven hours! We could not stop talking! We both left the restaurant wondering what had happened and what this all meant.

The week after, we met again for a large social event. I even planned an outfit to look cute for him! I had not felt that way in a very long time. At the event, I got some mixed signals. He did not know if I was interested and he was sort of awkward. He spoke to a lot of people and at the time, looked as though he was trying to get away from me. I left the party thinking he was simply a nice guy and was not particularly interested in me.

He followed up. He saw me the next day for a few minutes and made a date to meet me the day after. I knew he was on the same page as I was. He wanted to see where this could go.

That month, we continued to see each other on an increasingly consistent basis. The amount of days in between our meetings became less. We had a lot of fun. We made each other laugh. We talked a lot. It was fantastic.

Even with all of the amazing things happening in our new relationship, I was still afraid to kiss him. I liked him and I wanted it to be special but was afraid it would not live up to that expectation. It took a number of dates. When it happened, it was literally magical but that is a story for a different time. ☺

We moved in together three months after making it official. It worked for us. We were both working full time, and I was in school part time. We made it all work. It was not perfect, but we grew. We committed to working together as a team and this attitude continues to help us in any issue we come across.

Over the last few years, our relationship has experienced a lot of changes. This includes moving to a bigger place. I finished school, Peter started and completed his bachelor's. We both received promotions, Peter entered graduate school, and we got married. That is a lot for any relationship to experience in a few short years.

The reason that Peter and I are successful in all of these changes is because we communicate. We talk a lot. Sometimes that talking turns into a disagreement, but we work to resolve that disagreement. It does not always resolve itself in that moment and sometimes, we have the same disagreement multiple times. However, we are both committed to working through our disagreements.

I also have to be grateful for my previous relationships. I learned a lot through those experiences and this got me ready for my relationship with my husband. I learned the skills (yes skills) to make a relationship successful. Relationships do not have to be hard; they just require some work.

Romantic Relationships

TIPS & TRICKS

Communicate

**KEEP AN OPEN LINE OF COMMUNICATION
WITH YOUR PARTNER ABOUT EVERYTHING.**

Talk about the big (hopes, dreams, goals) and
small (the funny thing that happened to you
when you got your coffee in the morning)
things. Do not be afraid to have the hard
conversations. The hard conversations with
your partner will make your relationship grow.

Respect

ALWAYS RESPECT ONE ANOTHER.

This means emotionally, physically, mentally,
and spiritually.

ACTIVELY LISTEN TO THE NEEDS OF YOUR PARTNER.

Be engaged in the conversation and participate. You can miss a lot if you are not listening to what your partner is saying.

KNOW WHEN YOU ARE READY FOR A RELATIONSHIP.

If you are ready, then be open to a relationship. Do not sell yourself or the relationship short. If you are not ready, that is fine too. Just make sure you communicate that with yourself or your potential partner.

BE EACH OTHER'S SUPPORT SYSTEM

Be the first person cheering your partner on in their success. Be there for them in their tough times. Let your partner know you are in their corner 100%.

WORKSHEET

Feel free to answer the questions in a way you feel comfortable (ex. writing, drawing). *Get creative!*

. . . .

The most important thing in life is to learn how to give out love, and to let it come in.
- Morrie Schwartz

. . . .

What are your relationship goals?
(ex. stay single, get married, long term relationship)

_____

_____

_____

Why is this important to you?

_____

_____

_____

How close are you to achieving your relationship goals?

_____

_____

_____

What resources do you currently have to achieve your goal?

_____

_____

_____

What resources do you need in order to achieve your goal?

_____

_____

_____

When you reach your relationship goals you will be...

_____

_____

_____

What are your next steps towards your relationship goals?
List three steps that you will take.

_____

_____

_____

CHAPTER TEN

Work

I have had a few different jobs so far in my life. Most of my jobs have been in different industries. I have worked in a dermatologist's office, group homes, in catering, as a bank teller, and in various roles in higher education. Somehow all of these jobs lead me to my current profession as a college professor.

I began working when I was seventeen years old. I began working at a dermatologist's office. In this role, I got to learn a lot about skincare, the medical field, and working with different people. There was a family atmosphere in the office with all the employees. I also translated for Polish speaking patients. I loved the interaction with people, but this job helped me to realize the medical field was not for me. I did not mind the clerical side, of my job but I had no interest in the medical side of my job. It was a great job to have during my college years. I left the job when I had to commute to school to finish my degree.

After I completed college, I worked in the Human Services field. I worked in various group homes in my area. I always had a full-time job and a part time job to make extra money. This gave me the opportunity to work with different populations and for different agencies. At first, I was grateful to have a job soon after graduating college. I had the opportunity to learn a lot and meet new people. However, I quickly saw that this field is not the correct one for me.

I was experiencing burnout from working too many hours in different jobs. I also had a stronger desire to attend graduate school. I also wanted to do more in my job. I was trying to figure out how to make it all work. I was hesitant to leave my job at first and move in a new direction.

After my grandmother passed away, I made a sudden and abrupt decision to leave my job. I wanted to change my life and pursue my goals. I made the decision to go for it. The only problem was I made the decision, but I did not have a plan.

I was lost for a year. I had some jobs but nothing seemed to fit well. I was unsatisfied and unwilling to settle. The problem was that I did not know what I wanted.

In my transition time, I began working full time as a bank teller. I figured it was a way to have a full-time income while I tried to figure it out. Here, I was a confused woman in my mid-twenties working in the banking industry. It was a field that was completely new to me. I had no idea what I was doing.

As lost as I was, that transition time helped me. I got into graduate school and I had time to figure out where I wanted to be. I knew I wanted to work in higher education. The rest of the journey brought me to where I am today.

While I was in graduate school, I continued to have various jobs. This including working in college admissions, advising, and as a research assistant. In some cases, I did not get paid or I was paid very little. This was because I had to complete internships or needed the experience. At the time, I was not thrilled at the idea of little income but I now understand how this was helpful. This pattern continued for a few years while I worked through graduate school.

I became a full-time professor the last year of my twenties. Here I was, just under thirty years old, and working as a college professor. Most of my colleagues are at least a decade older than me if not more. I felt as though I made my dream a reality, but I was a bit scared.

I was a bit frightened at first. I experienced a bit of imposter syndrome in the beginning and I thought people could see right through me. In those moments, I was forgetting all of the hard work I had put in to achieve this goal. I forgot all the years of studying and sacrifice. I had earned this position.

I quickly finished my dissertation and became a doctor in my early thirties. I continued to receive training in different pedagogical methods. I redesigned curriculum. I became immersed in the field of teaching. I also continued to do research. I became so busy and focused that I did not realize how much I had accomplished. I quickly realized that I had developed a seven-page curriculum vitae.

In all of my seemingly unrelated work experiences, there is one thing I failed to realize. All of my jobs helped me to build a set of skills necessary in all of my jobs. I learned from each job. I figured out what I wanted to do and what I did not want to do. I also got lost in the process. While it was not pleasant at the time, it helped lead me to where I wanted to be.

The key is to find the area you are passionate about and then pursue the field. It may not be easy and it may not happen overnight. You may even need to work for free to gain experience (think internships). However, if it is where you want to be then it will all be worth it.

Work

TIPS & TRICKS

Network

CONTINUE TO NETWORK REGARDLESS OF WHAT STAGE OF YOUR CAREER YOU ARE IN.

Networking can lead to new collaborations or to your new job.

Get involved

FIND WAYS TO GET INVOLVED AT WORK.

Volunteer for extra events or projects. It is one way to get noticed at your jobs.

Keep training

FIND CONTINUING EDUCATION OPPORTUNITIES.

There are always new developments in every field and it is important to keep up with them. This can also improve your skills and make you stand out.

find Mentors

ONE WAY TO GROW IN YOUR GIVEN FIELD IS TO FIND MENTORS.

They can help guide and support you in your career. They can also help get you to the next level of your career.

WORKSHEET

Feel free to answer the questions in a way you feel comfortable (ex. writing, drawing). *Get creative!*

. . . .

Success is no accident. It is hard work, perseverance,
learning, studying, sacrifice and most of all,
love of what you are doing or learning to do.
- Pele

. . . .

What are your goals in work?
(ex. to make a lot of money, to make a difference, to become a CEO)

_____

_____

_____

Why is this important to you?

_____

_____

_____

How close are you to achieving your work goals?

_____

_____

_____

What resources do you currently have to achieve your goal?

_____

_____

_____

What resources do you need in order to achieve your goal?

_____

_____

_____

When you reach your work goals you will be...

_____

_____

_____

What are your next steps towards your work goals?
List three steps that you will take.

_____

_____

_____

_____

Closing Remarks
Let's keep the conversation going

It is my hope that "Progress not Perfection: A Millennial's Story" helped guide you towards your goals and dreams. Please continue to use this guide and review the goals that you have set in place. Once you achieve your goals then go back and set new ones. I know you will create the life that you desire!

The topics covered in this guided journal are just the beginning. There will be a new outlet to take these topics a step further. I am happy to share that this guided journal is turning into a podcast series. The Progress not Perfection with Dr. W. Podcast will continue the conversation that began in this guided journal. Tune in to the podcast to hear more topics, from guest speakers, and to contribute to the conversation!

I want to hear from you!

Share your copy of *"Progress not Perfection: A Millennial's Story"*

Connect & Share your photos with me
Instagram, Facebook, Twitter:
@BellesNotebook

Made in the USA
Monee, IL
16 February 2020